This book is to be returned on or before
the last date stamped below.

KEN SMITH

WILD ROOT

BLOODAXE BOOKS

Copyright © Ken Smith 1998

ISBN: 1 85224 461 5

First published 1998 by
Bloodaxe Books Ltd,
P.O. Box 1SN,
Newcastle upon Tyne NE99 1SN.

Bloodaxe Books Ltd acknowledges
the financial assistance of Northern Arts.

Cover printing by J. Thomson Colour Printers Ltd, Glasgow.

Printed in Great Britain by
Cromwell Press Ltd, Trowbridge, Wiltshire.

Our psyches seem to be so constructed that we need and desire an imagined "other" – either a glimmering, craved, idealised order, or another that is dark, savage and threatening.

– EVA HOFFMAN, *Exit into History*

Man is a battlefield...a dark cellar in which a well-bred spinster lady and a sex-crazed monkey are forever engaged in mortal combat, the struggle being refereed by a rather nervous bank clerk.

– D. BANNISTER, *Psychology as an exercise in paradox*

Every man is a master of disorder...

– CHRISTOPHER COLUMBUS, *Letter to the Sovereigns of Spain* (4th voyage)

I am the Emperor, and I want noodles.

– FERDINAND OF AUSTRIA, 1835-48

Acknowledgements

Acknowledgements are due to the editors of the following publications in which some of these poems first appeared: *Acumen, Ambit, Dog, The Echo Room, Hungarian Quarterly, Korunk* (Kolozsvár), *Mak* (Novi Pazaar), *New Statesman, Notre Dame Review, Orbis, Oxford Poetry, Poetry London Newsletter, Poetry Review, Poetry Wales, The Rialto, Stand, Stone Soup* and *Sunk Island Review.*

'Years go by' was published in *The Long Pale Corridor* (Bloodaxe Books, 1996); 'Bodycakes' and 'With a name like Spratt' appeared in *What Poets Eat* (Foolscap, 1995); 'Nights at the Blind Beggar' was in *Beyond Bedlam* (Anvil Press, 1997).

'Days on Dog Hill' was an outcome of the 1997 Ledbury Festival Squantum. 'Archive footage' was originally commissioned for *Kaleidoscope* (BBC Radio 4). 'No one' was commissioned by the South Bank on a theme of ghosts, and later broadcast on BBC Radio 4. *The Shadow of God, Wire through the heart* and *Eddie's other lives* were all commissioned and broadcast by BBC Radio.

Countryside around Dixton Manor is the title of a huge painting by an unknown artist displayed in the Cheltenham Art Gallery. The harvest verse is from *Five Hundred Points of Good Husbandry, 1580* by Thomas Tusser (OUP, 1984).

The opening section of *The Shadow of God* is adapted from the preamble to a letter written by Suleyman to Francis, King of France, to be found in Ernest Charrière's *Négociations de la France dans le Levant* (Paris, 1848).

Contents

EDDIE'S OTHER LIVES

Absent

The other half of the conversation
has flown off in a jetplane
to the country of her own tongue.

And maybe she'll come back to me
or maybe not or maybe she was all a dream
I had in the blue garden in the dusk.

In the house the TV is watching itself
and the stereo listening to itself
and the fridge with its running commentary.

She's out there. And I'm out here
among the moths and the last light,
the blackbird at her evensong.

Country music

In my other life in another country
on the world's other side I get by, just.

A little fishing a little hunting perhaps.
Maybe I'm a professor of aluminum siding

at Pork Chop U, an aficionado
of the beauties of felt roofing.

Let's say I drive a dusty brown pickup
with a roofrack and a rifle in the back.

What you're up against here is decay,
that in the system that makes it break down.

And anyway it's Friday. In all the arguments
for one more drink the ayes have it.

Therefore I'm on my way to the Captain's
to fill up the hole I've made in myself.

She's bored with me, I tired of her long ago.
We get by with the kids and the payments.

All the radio stations sing the same song:
love goes away, it's a sad tune

coming in over the airwaves and out
through the light years to the stars,

the same miserable message
to the whine of the same miserable guitar,

for forever or the next thing to it,
if anyone out there is listening.

Chief

On the one side my great great grandaddy
was Timuquana, chief in these parts.

A great hunter, woman chaser,
fighting man, joker, dreamer,

whose country was this where I work now
up and down the fairways and bunkers.

Look, here's his picture on the matchbook
from the country club of the same name:

the leathery face in the braids
and the one feather that breaks

out of the ring round him like a seal
on a document, his motto underneath:

Close cover before striking.
For safety strike on back.

When that cop come

Old Red we call him to his red face,
Hey Mister Red, Yes Sir Mister Red,
you see the heat rise to his head,
and that's what makes him crazy.

So then he's writing inside his hat
like he thinks it's New York,
Pay now pay later pay forever he says:
Gimme your name or I'll break your face.

Seems I remember him in school,
snot running down his white trash face,
a pimpled adolescent chewing toothpicks,
beating his meat behind the bandstand.

Now he's just a dirty cop in Meatville
writing my name down in his notebook
telling me I'm booked, hooked, cooked,
and I'm telling him *this conversation cut.*

Joy #1

Come down here this mornin Madson Wisconsin goin home Denver. Husban's up there inna Vetrans Hospital Madson, s'real good hospital.

He got hit by a truck. Half his face smashed in, one eye hangin out. Couldn't look at him.

Had to make myself. Asked me how I look Joy? I said OK Sonney. It was a goddamn lie. Looks like shit. No wonder I'm smokin like they goin outa style.

In the next street

There's only ever one argument: his,
bawling out whoever punctuates
the brief intervals his cussing
interrupts, something unheard, reason perhaps.

What you never get is silence,
always some groan on the horizon
out on the borders of attention
where would be quiet if they let it.

Always some conversation far away,
foreign, banal, dramatic, translated
it means *my wife's name is Judit.*
I am an engineer from Spidertown.

What to reply? *Your Majesty*
my name is Smith. All lies anyway,
all we do is get drunk, the evening's end
collapsing loosely into gutturals.

We drink to silence, where the stars think.
We drink to the music of rain on the roof.
We drink to mothers, brothers, lovers, kids,
to the candle burning down its length

till someone blows it out. Distance
makes no difference, the same want
for love and money, the numbers of the winning line
in the state lottery like a needle in the brain.

And then I've had enough. I want
to go home now, far away, plug myself
back into the sockets, the blackbird,
the evening humming stories to itself.

Everything in its place, the moths,
the mouse in the mousetrap. And
in the next street the same old argument.
He's sure he's right.

Joy #2

My mother. She was killed onna street. Had t'go home to Livpool England bury her. That's where I come from, ways back. She was killed right onna street, hit by car. Knocked down hit an run. She was onna crossing. She was dead. She was inna right. But she was dead.

Poem to which the answer is no

This music you're listening to –
let me tell you why I don't like it.

No.

You with your pretty little Doris Day wife.
She's been buying and selling in cyberspace.
She's looking at Jesus through the eyes of Bugs Bunny.

And *yes*. This could be me here among the glittering cities,
Eddie the Unsteady glimpsed travelling in the opposite direction
on an Amtrak out of Toledo, last heard from in a motel room
in Moon Township, old curmudgeon on a stick
limping aimless in America, through all the other zones
of time and distance and the self, beautifully lost
somewhere in the great riddle of nowhere, my double,
carbon copy, fax, living on my wits, conjuring
something out of nothing and taking that to the bank.

I'm sorry sir, we're not connected to that service.
Your call cannot be completed as dialled.

Eddie's on the hoof,
Eddie's off the bone,
Eddie's getting drunk
and won't come to the phone.

More stick

Here he comes again my man Eddie,
making his way downtown on some cross street,
the rain and the cold wind in his face
down past Jerry's barber shop and shoe shine
on his way to the invisible liquor store.
Like me he is of the brotherhood of men
with sticks. *East Wacker to West Wacker*
six times a day and back again, I was
a messenger then my foot got sick.
it collapsed goddammit. Eddie on the edge
of everything, Eddie on a freight train
to a heart attack. He can say
you're the one who was here, always will be.
He can say only time I refused a drink
I misunderstood the question. Oh he can talk,
he's the epicentre of any conversation,
it runs all round him but he's not here
and tomorrow won't remember. Any of it.

And through it all the dead music
of the buildings, airshafts and ventilators
and the electrics, the sirens hunting down
the streets of the trashed neighbourhoods
along the lake shore, scruffy trees
standing in black water, then just the gleam
of cities shining in the night, blur
of conversations over the Earth's rim.

This is a fugue that is a dream of the world
that's a bad dream anyway. *Fool:*
what's this fist for, this automatic
in your guts, this knife? Fact is
in this bar he's come in from the rain to,
waiting for a train or a bus or a plane,
fact is there's not one not two not three
but four talking TV screens competing
for his anxieties. All this infests his brain.

But Eddie no crazy. Eddie sick, he in trouble
but he no lose it. Eddie no mad.

Joy #3

Name's Joy, an that's my nature. But I swear to God it gets harder. Don't much get on with Sonney's two boys from first marriage, 16 and 18 years old, both of them crazy, crazy as lunes, out half the night raisin hell, come home, switch on TV stereo high as it'll go.

Sonney wants me to move up there with them, thinks he'll be there a while. Says he wants me with him but I don't know, sella house, move our stuff, get those boys to help an I don't know they will.

Joy #4

When I married my first husban Elliot I was a GI bride. Those days I was an entertainer, I was a stripper, clubs inna north, Leeds, Manchester. I thought he was the sweetest thing. We didn't last. People don't I guess. His business went broke an he took off, took a farm up in South Dakota, took the boy. I said I wouldn go, said I didn come here to be no farmer's wife out inna wilderness, so we split.

The geography of clouds

It all happens so fast, in the long grass
looking up, or staring from the bus
going West: the stately kingdoms of the clouds

collapsing into violent republics, empires
forming and fading on fast forward.
The cartographers never catch up,

the mapmakers turn broody and suicidal,
the subtitles in an unknown tongue,
white on white and all too fast.

In a half an afternoon the history of Russia,
in an hour the discovery and conquest of the New World,
in minutes the development of moveable type.

The late bloom is on the sedge
reads the soundtrack. *And the blossom*
no sooner flowers than it falls.

East of here, west of here

the days are the great flatlands,
long arc of the earth's curve
falling away on all points of the compass.

And what the light presents: barn, tree,
girl in an orchard, an old woman
peeling apples, glimpsed as you go.

The nights are the mountains,
to be got through in the headlights
east of the river or west of the watershed:

the same: speech that make sense
only of essential things: bread and salt
in greeting, a glass of wine, farewell,

some place to lay me down to sleep
to the tick of the same bedside clock,
the battery wearing itself away.

Noises off

Some dream or other, the moon wash
through the window blinds, the night city
with its night sounds. I'm on the road again
in my other life, the lights glittering
in the late distance, the wind
broken out of Canada and laced with sleet.

So here I am in this little town
between ocean and ocean with my bag
and my out of state cheques and no cash.
I'm rich in bad paper and dead currency
and they say *money never lies idle*
but what do they know of it?

It's always this aching hour of the night
in some place called French Lick
or Mud City Indiana, the connection
half a day away to some unhappy town
where the furniture is made of neon
and sings in praise of K-Mart and the 7-11.

And there is always racket, machinery
that bleeps to say your dinner's done,
your laundy's dry, horns, talking trucks,
the chatter of the video arcades
and the low murmer of the soaps
and the endless wailing of the cops.

Alarms no one ever answers, bells
that ring till the electricity runs out,
and then a door opens on a sudden blast
of heartbreak music, betrayal's beat,
the same old blues of separation,
men's inconsistencies and women's.

Joy #5

Don't know what I can do in Madson. Waitressin I guess. Just when I was thinking to live and die in Denver now I have to do the same for Wisconsin. I don't know.

Sonney was driving to Canada, got hit up there by Green Bay. Hit by truck. He looked awful, don't know how he's gonna look when it's over.

Kept askin me How do I look Joy, how do I look? It's real good hosptal.

He was smashed up before. Phtographer. In Veetnam got a grenade in his back, thirty seconds get it out with a fish hook. Goddamm Veetcong.

Speech

Now America is one whirled fire,
one babble of speech, the captions loosed
from the cartoons, the sentences
issuing out of the wrong mouths:

fuck you says Chief Joseph,
throwing down his spanner, fired
within six months of his pension
from the Milwaukee Cutout Corporation.

One more nightshift, leaves the bar
and torches the factory. Out in the wind
that picks at the stone face of the city
for the last time in this life

Schroeder stomps to his pickup:
from where the sun now stands,
punching the radio to country,
I will fight no more forever.

A dream of disaster

Now where we are we will always be,
the moon high on second hand light,
her dark weight lugging the tides
between ebb line and nepe.

We never got there, driving through Ohio
when the brakes failed, someone
pulled a gun, or in the airspace
of the wide Atlantic some instrument

gave in to entropy and heaved us seaward.
We are the names on the lists.
This is our baggage floating in the sea.
We are the percentage of the reckoning.

And the moon up there is our crazy sister
who just never got started, and we
are on our way to join the angels
in their interminable barbershop quartets.

Dead trousers

Old trousers that were best once, now
they never go anywhere, mooching round the house
doing odd jobs, paint and varnish stains,
urine and spilt coffee where once was beer,
whisky, the faint aroma of sex on the hoof.

So the centuries flash by: all those handsome women
in pretty dresses that turn suddenly black.
And the impossible jobs: making a whole
of the hole in yourself, slamming the door
on your discontent and out into the rain.

You're on hold, in the queue, listening
to the *Nessun dorma* song on the line
and the *sorry-to-keep-you-waiting* voice,
faint electronics at the world's rim.
Please speak after the tone.

Please leave your name and number. Speak.
Get it all off your chest: love and love's
bereavement and how short a term of office.
Make your confessions, all the bloody times
you were a bloody fool. So speak.

To nobody out there.

The theft

I am a thief and this my thiefwork,
here in the rare book room in Toledo
rummaging the works of the dead professors,
examining their boxes of effects.

It comes to this: a stout carton
in which the late dean's ashtray, gown,
seal of office, rotary inscription,
pipe, golf trophy and cigar-cutter.

Amen.

Joy #6

*I guess I'll do it all just like he says. My friend
Marlene, she waitresses with me, real good friend,
she'll help me I know.*

*When my mother got killed onna crossing she said
she'd come with me, help out, I said no. Strange
goin back there. Hadn't been in 40 years, hadn't
seen my mother since don't know. But she was dead,
so I just buried her, came away, nothing else to do
but come on home.*

The telephone is in the key of C

she says, breathless, home again
from the long corridors of air and traffic
over the ocean's curve, where I have prayed
to all the gods of wind and water

for her safe return, keeping the stillness
still for her. The stories tumble
over each other, interrupt each other,
all she's met, ate, heard, trembled at

in the country of endless explanations
and too many sudden noises, the freeways
and the announcements yelling in her skull
from the continent of her own tongue.

All falling away, almost in her grasp,
a word forming in the ear of her hearing,
glimpsed in the moment that's gone now,
the stray bullet snug in its target.

In the year of the comet, with vodka,
phenobarb and plastic bags on their heads
39 grownups went off to board the UFO,
each with a roll of quarters for the shuttle.

The telephone is in C. And the dryer,
that's just a basso profundo klaxon
that won't quit, that and the microwave,
that and the cuckoo clock and the planes.

Sleep is what she needs, and a dream
through which geese on the inlet,
near and then distant, fading south
beyond the night swamps into summer.

The rustle of magnolia in the wind
and the stars over all, a nightbird
calling over water, the oncoming
of the great trains' wild concertos.

28

Before the Lisbon tribunal

They asked why I came here. I replied
to hear the rain falling in the street,
footsteps running into the wet dark.
To consume fish and more fish, drink tinto,
branco, verde, secco, make love, sleep late,
waking to the calls of ships on the Tagus.

And the arrival of what ships did I wait for?

I described the *Alfama* winding on itself,
a heap of washing lines and lemon trees,
sardine scales underfoot, children tumbling
down its alleys. In the cold empty cathedral
what I felt was *cold, empty*, a barn
built by the thugs of the Second Crusade.

What could I tell them of this?

I spoke of *Guincho*, its name that means scream
for the Atlantic wind rushing through, days
watching the slow shift in the quick sea
arriving in walls of water, the sea's change
and the light's change till the round bowl
of the earth's rim's lost and the light gone.

And where did I think such light went?

They were amused, patient. Those were early days,
I was not yet accused. At my second examination
they were seven, young, clever, soft spoken,
a clerk scratching, his tongue between his teeth.
There were no charges, the questions random:
could a ship of armed men be hidden in a fist?

Did I believe their mares sired by the West Wind?

Did cheese produce mites, bad meat blowflies,
did a closed box of old rags generate mice?
I was to help clear up certain allegations,
they as anxious as I, and so forth, to be done.
I have pen, ink, paper, candle, a writing desk
and this white room wherein to write my confessions.

Poem without a title

The borders are open,
the borders are closed.

I stood in a long line of suitcases
in the Hall of Tears. Each
they inspected in leisurely detail,
quartering the face, solemn.

Sullen. *Open please.* I recall
a pair of blue women's underpants
held to the grubby satin of the neon,
and the paperwork, the paperwork, I thought

this time they will empty out
the entire suitcase of my heart
when Bang went the rubber stamp,
and Klik the Ausgang. *Go now* they said.

Into the gold light. Into the birdsong of the dollar,
into the constellation of the milkshake.
Go be the little boy that lives in the lane,
this is what you get for your sack of apples.

Still he was there, my father,
at the stair's end these twenty years,
back from the shadow country saying again *I told you so*
I told you so.

*

The salt in the shaker,
pepper in the pot, everything
in its place here at the Terminal Café:
eggs on the skillet, coffee in the cup.

Outside the river traffic on the river,
the sky as the sky is, blue if you will.
I can stroll in the Italian Gardens,
I can relax in the Sicilian Colonnade.

Here in the city I'm at home.
This is what I get for all my apples.
There's a bar I go to.
There's a woman I see.

There's a bridge where I watch
dusk after dusk the downgoing sun
lash the water to fire, and go home
content in the dark and recall nothing.

*

Years go by

Father I say. Dad? You again?
I take your arm, your elbow,
I turn you around in the dark and I say

go back now, you're sleep walking again,
you're talking out loud again, talking in tongues
and your dream is disturbing my dream.

And none of this is any of your apples,
and even now as the centuries begin to happen
I can say: go away, you and all your violence.

Shush, now, old man.
Time to go back to your seat in the one-and-nines,
to your black bench on the Esplanade,

your name and your dates on a metal plate, back
to your own deckchair on the pier, your very own
kitchen chair tipped back on the red kitchen tiles

and you asleep, your feet up on the brass fender
and the fire banked, your cheek cocked
to the radio set, this is the 9 o'clock news Dad.

It's time. It's long past it.
Time to go back up the long pale corridor
there's no coming back from.

Part of the crowd that day

They watched the pilgrims leave for Santiago
gawping by the roadside. In the harbour
watching the boats gather they knew something
was afoot, so many horses and these armed men.
Mostly it was all too difficult to believe.
They watched the stones rise in the cathedral.
They watched the stars. They watched winter
follow summer and the birds fly south again.
They watched the thieves carted up the road
to Tyburn and the beggars whipped through town.
They were townsfolk, craftsmen, shopkeepers,
the labouring poor who came in from the fields.
They watched the witches burn, the heretics.
They watched the ships leave for the Americas.
They were on the bridge at Sarajevo the first time.
They saw. They wondered. They shouted
burn her, hang him, slaughter the Albigensians.
They were the onlookers, the crowd a gasp runs
mouth to mouth down the grumbling street
as Marie Antoinette goes by, and this time
they are shouting for her head. There goes
the Iron Duke, there the beaten Corsican,
and this the little father of all the Russians,
this the firing squad. They were on the hills
looking down on burning Rome, and still around
when Il Duce came to town, and how they cheered.
They gawp at the hungry, they gawp at the dead.
In the end they are not spared. In their turn
everything happens to them. Of any half dozen
one has a secret vice, one an incurable disease,
one a deep faith in God and the rest don't care
one way or the other. But they see it all happen.

With a name like Spratt

Imagine at their dinner if you will
Jack and Mrs Spratt, whose name was Martha,
may she rest in peace and all the saints preserve us.

Née Robinson. Sole relict Jeremiah Bethia Robinson,
a man that was never any fun at breakfast,
a life from start to finish without meat and 2 veg.

You will recall his long face spouting God's holy word
at every spoonful of his pudding, an upright
exclamation of a man much given to kneeling down.

As was Martha. When Jack took her he would take her
from behind and call it prayer, wondering the while
what's for supper, wondering if the stars were edible.

He loved her for her bones. He did this or that
and one died then the other and they're long gone now
to where there's nothing in the cupboard but the dark.

Theirs was a tale told to cheer the poor
and promote thrift among the lower classes.
Written on their stone *They licked the platter clean.*

Suspicion of reporters

Help she was howling over and over,
a long call in fire and he:
he was scribbling *help me
I'm burning*, his mind's eye

setting angle, speed, distance,
closing the shutter, the bright
ring of strangeness around things
forming the frame of her burning.

He wrote *Nor could I save her*,
he that was chronicler, eye
of events at their centre. As she
in her death was, as this is.

White noise

Late night watching TV till it stops.
The hiss silence sings to the ear
carried in on the electron blizzard
patching into uneasy sleep.

Slow panic of walking columns
tents blown on the wind
shifting the lost villages
in shoes those who have shoes.

Bringing the desert along with them
its seeds in the mattock's edge
in the hoe's angle those who have hoes
bringing their hot rainless weather.

Call me Shrug I know nothing.
I'm like distant trouble. I may be
far from your door but I know
your name and address, alias and alibi.

Will our children bear children
and will they be anyone like us?
Will the great stream shift south
will the rain come will the ice?

You say one day but name it: *Tuesday
the fifth sixth the fifteenth
October November December*. Your life flies past
like a train and you're on it.

Body Cakes

(for Aggie, recalling Asa)

Öländska kroppkakor. Kroppkakor.
He liked to say it, aloud, over and over,
reciting his recipe of white flour,
barley flour, potato flour, potatoes,
onion and allspice. One of his ceremonies
that end to end made up a life: his.
Or just what he wanted to eat.

I never cooked them but the once,
the same rainy day I watched
his tall skinny body into the narrow grave
dug too short so they must tip him,
I thought his black cap perched on the coffin
would slither away, but it stayed.

We got on with the bitter ritual
of burying the man I loved.
It rained all that day and that night
we got drunk, and we sang *please
keep me in your dreams.* He was
gone from me, my viking, *vicarunga,*
my long lover, whose boat came ashore
here on my life so long ago now,
and from there I was stilled.

The body cakes weren't a success,
grey, a mush, wallpaper paste,
that the next day early, before anyone
rose from their beds, I took out
and buried, deep, in the garden.

Archive footage

The film is jumpy in the sprockets, bleached
in black and white and all the shades of grey.
The memory is dying. Look: this is Jack,
in the fading photo cracking at the corners.

The seaswell, the old grey swilltub
filling in the first milky light with grey ships,
so many manoeuvring in so much silence. Jamey?
Jimmy or was it Jack? The sky another grey.

Jammy we called him for he was lucky.
He'd been in Africa in tanks, the one man out
when the magazine blew and all his mates gone.
They put him back together. Jerry.

George? He'd gotten wed, they had 36 hours
of Withernsea passion in a mate's caravan.
They sky bleached out. Here the shoreline
of dune and shingle, flat country over the seawall.

John? Joey? Jim? Home the last time turning
at the back kitchen door, his handprint
pressed into the wet blue paintwork. That
she kept thereafter, that was all of him.

Photographs say nothing. Cheekyface
she called him. And he liked his beer.
Years from now she'll sing again
she'll dream again we'll meet again.

And there'll be bluebirds. Jess. Jeff.
5th East Yorks wet and seasick off La Rivière.
Shot or drowned, face down in the sea,
his white enamel mug drifting after him.

Years from now the wireless becomes the radio,
the gramophone the record player
and the record player the stereo, she'll sing along
songs he sang her then, his lily and his rose.

Josh. Johnny. Jock. The memory is dying,
the battery running flat. Before it fades
let's say this one is for Jimmy and for Jack,
and all the others who are never coming back.

First and last, Alderney

(for Judi)

Nights with the sea's mouth at my ear,
the moon at the window. Each day
the beach flushed twice over,
newly minted with footprints.

All day walking, Platte Saline,
La Bonne Terre, up the Zigzag
to Giffoine, to the Four Winds
and La Vieille Terre and the town.

Gulls. Distance that's one side
Normandy, the other wild Atlantic
pouring itself in, the northeaster
that rips up all our words,

all he said and she said
and all they meant: the tale
that's merely you and I my love,
weary and adrift and wordless

at the light's end, at supper
in the First and Last where we are
sole audience to some tipsy crew
wondering aloud whither the weather

and whether the weather wizard works.
She says it's all too blue out there
and all too blue in here. She says
I wish to God I'd never fallen down those bloody stairs.

He says he rather likes the idea of a ratdog.
And so forth. And as for me
I was getting my voice back from the wind,
trying to keep it to myself, I was

thinking how we could be nothing much,
grass in the restless air, a high bird
rising in the baymouth in a landscape
with the light bleeding out of it.

I want to sit here in this moment
of the quick world and watch
the light fall over the long seawall,
the sea beating at the harbour mouth.

I want to be who I want, the wind
rocking me to sleep till I'm still.
I want to be in love with water
and seaweed and lost shoes and you,

taking serious interest in the tides
and the moon's battered face, the gale
banging at itself, the casual dramatics
of the way the world works out.

The way each day the tide makes
a clear heart's shape in the bay's arc.
You the gulls mutter overhead
their cries rising in the last light:

you, you. I can be glad anyone
makes anything at all of anything,
in whatever space there is,
any shape on the delicate air will suffice.

Poem for translation

He loves a woman. If she lived
on the other side of the street
he would cross the traffic to her.
If she lived on the other side of the city
herd take a bus, take a train, call a taxi.

If she lived on the other side of the river
he'd take the ferry, row a boat, he could swim
to her, waiting on the riverbank as he arrives,
dripping wet, with a flower in his teeth,
his tongue working at the first words of her language.

If she lived on the other side of the ocean
he would work, beg, borrow or steal,
and fly to her. But it's not like that.

She lives on the other side of a closed border,
in a country without visas or passports
or any kind of paperwork. They would be
closer if she lived on the other side of the moon.
She would be more alive to him if she were dead.

It's as if she exists on the other side of music
or birdsong, on the other side the mirror,
close but far away, like an echo. She's the song
he doesn't have words to, the words he has no tune for,
almost the melody he can almost hear.

For Julia, 1910-1996

Tears, like the rain falling, like
the first pale flowers opening in spring,
oh such a surprise. And then
the full riot of tears, beauty, weather,
before the leaves begin falling again.

But this time the whole tree has fallen
with a great echo and scurry through the forest.

That's the way she went: with wind and stormclouds
and nine days of rain, and over East Ham
Town Hall a double rainbow, and no doubt
at each foot of it a whole crock of gold
for anyone foolish enough to look for it.

There's always an end, has to be,
an end to everything, to summer
and to rain, to love even.
And to the endless sketch of the conversation
in the head – if you remember it aright,
if it ever took place, ever happened at all –
even if it's just a conversation
you only imagined, longed for, for years,
with this woman everyone loved.

Dead now, and so far beyond all our desires,
said or unsaid, all of it the same now
in the broad length and the long breath.

All I can say is: let the heart fill,
let it flood with love, till it bursts.
What else is there?
                    Death, my friends,
is a dark blood red wine, that comes
in a tall green bottle, a Rioja from Spain,
or a Merlot from somewhere abouts Balaton,
with a label that is but one small corner
of a Csontváry painting: Mary at the Well,
circa 1908: women come for water,
on their elegant heads great clay pitchers
borne aloft with such tall, timeless, eloquence.

Looking for the constant

(for Alan Sandage, astronomer)

It was the best of all possible lives,
much spent lying night after black night
in the hard cold cradle on the mountain
under the 200", gawping like a boy again –

the same boy with his ear to the telephone pole,
listening for the singing through the wires
of words in the wood – staring into the stars,
further and further out among the jewels of time.

The life of an eyeball. A life of measuring,
allowing angle, age, velocity and distance,
the black dusts, warps, city haze, and all of it
in motion, afloat, aloof, in orbit with itself –

and with whatever else lies out beyond the faint
limit we can barely see where for us the lights
aren't lit yet, on their long tether to infinity –
watching the far galaxies breathe into the plates.

It was an honourable life, a long tradition
fore and aft of those who wondered why
and what is all this stuff? It was a dreaming,
seeking a measure in the unforgiving distances –

crouched in my cold cage among the stars
from which we're all of us made – and I was
part of that becoming, nothing endeavouring
to be something that could understand itself.

The rest was cold calculation: maps, papers,
surveys. I sought a constant, the ratio
of speed to mass that meant creation
thinned forever to grow dark and silent –

or collapsed and blew apart again,
the breathing out of breathing in,
a symmetry. There might be reason there,
if not a god of love a god of meaning.

At any rate that's the scenario I go for.

No one

*Let no one be surprised at what we are about to relate, for it was common
gossip up and down the countryside that after February 6th many people
both saw and heard a whole pack of huntsmen in full cry. They straddled
black horses and black bucks while their hounds were pitch black with star-
ing hideous eyes. This was seen in the very deer park of Peterborough town,
and in all the woods stretching from that same spot as far as Stamford. All
through the night monks heard them sounding and winding their horns. Reli-
able witnesses who kept watch in the night declared that there might well
have been twenty or even thirty of them in this wild tantivy.*

    – from the *Anglo-Saxon Chronicle,* 1127

Voices in empty rooms, in the time that is no time
beyond midnight, a shape in the milky moonlight,
a pattern of shadow, the chill column of air
on the landing. No one there. No one.

Thuds in the dark, and from the locked room
a groan, whether of pain or passion, then the nothing
we go on listening to. Cats. The building sinking
into itself, dry rot eating the timbers. Spooks.

No one's here. Ghosts. The dead who are dead
and for nothing, tangled like smoke.
Ghosts of the barbed wire that persists
long after the rain and the rust has eaten all its teeth.

To all this the stars pay no attention.
To each came the night of the last syllable
and its endless pointless repetition,
a water that remembers all that's passed through it.

Ghosts of my grandfather's white shirts
on the wind through the washing lines,
his voice that still says whenever I visit him
I hope you've had your tea we've just had ours.

Misty ghosts of the rain falling in the last of the forest
up by Theydon Bois, the dead ferns and the weeping birch,
and the old voices rubbing through like stains,
the same refusals spinning down the cortex.

47

The ghosts of meaning in the mouths of politicians.
Ghosts of the job I don't have, every day
I go down and clock on though I never get paid
still it keeps the hands and feet busy

and you know the monkey likes to use his hands and feet.
I have become the upturned hook at the question's end,
the maker of one syllable at a time: *moon moon.*
I am the ghost of the actor who only ever played ghost.

Ghosts. Vanished peoples consigned to the hedgebacks,
their gods demoted to the production of sour milk.
There are countries that don't exist any more, citizens
with their wines and their sauces and their music

where are now new people with their different names,
the Road of Brotherhood & Unity become the Avenue of Victories.
Of the language of the butchering Huns a single word remains
and that *strava*, meaning funeral, all they left behind.

Ghosts.

Half mad and half wild, there are times if I don't go crazy
I'd go crazy, so I'm walking in the dawn and the traffic
all the way to Barking asking where has the silver river
of my voice babbled off to? Calling in the ghosts.

Whoever they are they will not go down the river,
they drift like the drowned bride in the water eddy,
returning over and over to count the takings,
scraping their knives across the doorstone.

Ghosts.

In the new minted year 1091 the priest Walchelin
taking his customary homeward path through the woods
was assailed by the howling of the homeless dead
led by a man with clubs, *exercitus mortuorum.*

Familia Herlechini, Gabriel's hounds: the wings
of the wild geese overhead, mist shapes, lights on the moor,
then the onrush of the wild hunt, soldiers and women,
the parson and the clerk, the lovers who will never be satisfied.

Ghosts.

Once on Alderney I glimpsed through rain and sea-squall
where their miserable burials had been the graveyard
of the slaves who were whipped there and were all called *Russ.*
Nothing there. No one. That side is all golf now,

bunkers of one sort or another, rainy emplacements
where the field lines were broken, gun turrets
knotted in briar and seagrass, the road curves away
through the few trees it takes to make a wood there.

Years ago a young man in blue across the porch, a clear
afternoon in Pennsylvania, solid, adolescent,
loping by the long windows, and then he jumped
into the bushes and was gone. No one there,

at the rope's end the dog flailing the empty air.
There had been such a boy, sulky, slamming his machine
into the oncoming traffic on the turnpike. Once.
And this was his short cut, mooching into town.

Another that stepped tread by long heavy tread
down the stairs of my father's house, and the door
slammed so the house shook and we woke and we looked
but the bolts lay home, the key snug in its socket.

We agreed, my father and I. No one there.
It was all we ever agreed. Now he's long gone
into the dark, to whatever answer to whatever question,
incommunicative as he ever was, and still angry.

Dead and buried, there was the cut glass bowl,
its silver rim cracked all the way around, the sound of it
high in the air of Sunday afternoon tea and that because
there was no place at the table for him, he was dead dammit.

That and two words that came clear, roundabout, devious,
distorted on the telephone, garbled in translation –
and a knock, once, at the back kitchen door,
the shape of him as if he would come in from the night.

But no one. My mother stands at the door looking out
and he's not there, the kitchen light scatters outward
on the path and the dusty leaves of the blackcurrant bushes.
And now she's dead, little Milly, but of her not a glimmer.

Not much at all of her: the ring she wore I wear,
her button box, thimbles, pins, a card of hooks, a grey
length of cotton threaded through a needle's eye,
a white china shoe with the arms of the city of Blackpool.

Goodbye she says, rouged and pretty and pink
in her stout wooden box. *Goodbye.*
She'd say *I've seen better on a card of buttons.*
She'd say *You make your bed you lie in it.*

Sometimes I almost hear her, where the stair turns,
or I almost see her as I pick the bright black berries
year by year on the cuttings from her garden by the sea,
few as they are each summer there are more of them.

Countryside Around Dixton Manor, *circa* 1715

Now strike up drum
cum harvest man cum.
Blowe horne or sleapers
and cheere up thy reapers

Layer under layer under the paintwork
England is making its Midsummer hay –

the dancing morris, pipelads and drum,
scythemen and rakers, cockers and carters

and centrefield my lord with his ladies
riding where now the pylon hums

with its wires over spring wheat
through the morning's early mist.

These are the same hedgebacks,
same lie to the landscape, Mickle Mead,

Barrowdine, Harp Field and Sausage
still here though the names are gone now.

* *

In oils, unsigned, anonymous, a jobber
moving through landscape, used maybe
the wide angle lens of the *camera obscura*
for this sweep of a corner of Gloucestershire,

back when all was thought well enough,
and nothing would change beyond this –
these peasants sweating in harvest
content dreaming brown ale and a fumble

among the haycocks, and the dancers dance off
to their drink and their shillings. My lord lies now
and since and soon and thereafter in Alderton
in St Mary of Antioch, long dead.

* *

51

Long gone, nameless maids in a row,
long curve of the back of 23 men
in a Mexican wave of swung scythes

to their lost graves. Two gossips
by the gate that is still a gate
maybe went for infantry, and the pipeboy

shipped out to the far world, most
stayed, went hungry, died anyway.
The painting's a lie, the landscape true

where the field keeps its shape. Everything
beyond this moment is yet to happen.
Everyone here is part of the dust now.

* *

If my heart aches it's for this
though none of it's true:

the world we have lost never was
so we never lost it:

glitter of horse brass, bells
rolling over the evening:

all my lord's dream of himself
in a hired man's painting:

same tale then as now
and this has not changed either:

the enriching of the rich –
impoverishment of the poor.

None but the reaper
will come to your door.

The Great Hat Project

(for JHW, may he thrive and with him all his ilk & tribe)

Hats I have known: the broad brimmed,
the beaked, the peaked, the high crowned,
the aviator's leather helmet with flaps,
the beret cocked at an angle to the brow,
the hat at ease with itself, the top hat,
the hard hat, the clown's cap and bells,
the Homberg, the silk, the stetson, the straw,
the Derby, the wide brimmed curé's hat
that drifted away from me from the iron bridge
long ago; the hood, the helmet, the ten-gallon,
the sou'wester, the rain hat, the sun hat,
the biretta, the busby, the bearskin,
the Sherlock Holmes, the Napoleonic full fig,
the beanie, the porkpie, cutiepie,
paper hat, party hat, kiss-me-quick hat,
the mitre, the flat cap, the black cloth
worn by the judge sentencing a man to hang
by the neck and may God have mercy on his soul;
the blue baseball cap worn brim backwards,
the bobble with a badge *Georgia Bulldogs,*
the pith helmet, the shapka, the turban,
the tarboosh, the fez and the liripipe
all of which I must wear when I want to be invisible.

And oh the fedoras of victory, the trilbies of shame,
the kerchiefs of desire, the beavers of lust,
the cloche, mantilla, chenille, chaperon, Phrygian cap.
Hosannah to the panamas of innocence, hallelujah
to the bonnets of bliss, aloh al-akbar
to the cachic and the bashlik and the burnous,
hats off to the scarves of the babushkas.
Did you know Lincoln wrote the Gettysburg Address
sitting on a train using his stovepipe hat
as a desktop? What do you think of that?
The hat as mine-of-out-of-the-way-information.
Signor Know-it-all. Magister Clever Chops.
The hat's bona fides. Hat's old bones.

The hat public enemy number one, pariah,
persona non grata. Hat the subversive.
Hat the arbiter of impeccable taste and discrimination.
The stocking cap treatment. The hat puzzle.
The great sombrero scandal of September 1895.
The hat tax. The War of the Seven Blue Bonnets.
The hat nightmare. The everlasting unforgiving
memory of hats, their absolute refusal to compromise.
The nine lives of hats. The transcendence of hats.
The hat's birthplace in Galilee removed overnight
by the physical intervention of angels, deposited
lock, stock, stall, manger, halter and harness
in the grotto at Loretto, according that is
to Pauline theosophy, can you swallow that?
Night of the long hats. Hats in outer space.
The hat worn by Those Who Do Great Works.
The polkadot hats of the Sublime Insurrectionists.
The pointy hats worn by professors of pontification
at the university of Chapeau Falls Wisconsin
in the Department of Missing Headgear,
Faculty of Hat Studies. Hat and mouth disease.
The flora and fauna of hats. Hats Rule OK.
The hat in the poetry of Andrew Locomotion.
A Short Treatise on the Hat, by Harry Novak.
The It'll-be-all-right-on-the-night hat.
The hats of God. The Great Hat of Versailles.
Imagine the hat made of water, the hat made of snow.
The people's hat is deepest red. Electrification
plus hats equals the revolution. The silly hat brigade.
Give me liberty or give me hats. Hats off to Larry.
Into the valley of hats rode the six hundred.
Two acres and a hat. We take these hats to be self-evident.
The hat soliloquy: Whether to take up arms
against a sea of hats and by opposing end them,
that is the question. For every hat a season, a farewell.
For every hat there is an opposing hat. Hat=mc^2.
The silly girls' night out hat. The pig's hat.
The lumpenproletarian hat. The great hat famine.
The heroic hat. The destabilised hat.
The deconstructed postmodernist hat.
The hat as a concept just at the edge of meaning.

Yawning, he wonders if it's time for bed yet.
And can he please have his dinner now?
Portrait of *The Hat with Fish and Apples*.
Painting of the hat in robes of the Bishop of Durham.
Hat in the role of Lear. Hat son-of-a-bitch.
The hat visits an ailing relative in Caerphilly.
Suddenly the hat sits bolt upright in his rocking chair.
The hat on the wintery Haf drinking mulled wine.
Photo of the hat in his garden by the runner beans.
Hat, star of stage and screen. Hat son of Hat
who was begotten of Hat from a long and noble lineage
reaching back into the Bronze Age, the Neolithic,
who knows? Hat's escutcheon, his entire dog and pony show.
The hat realizes *Jesus I'm somebody's father*.
The hat fights in the Spanish war on the wrong side.
The hat's nemesis. Sometimes the hat makes love
to his sister and later is devoured by guilt,
this despite the fact hats have no genitals.
Adolf's hat, the goosestepping *Sieg heil* hat.
Nacht und Nebel hat. Ein Reich ein Hut.
The hats of the ethnic cleansers, caps worn
around Pale by some calling themselves poets,
their manicured haircuts that are also hats.
Hat bastards. The hat in the underworld,
realising what he's capable of in the name of hat.
The hat as envisaged by Dante in the 7th ring of hell.
The hat is a Dutchman far away from home.
The hat asking the whereabouts of the red light district.
The hat smuggling in a little hashish via his hatband.
The get-stuffed hat. The go-boil-your-head hat.
The am-I-making-enough-of-an-asshole-of-myself-yet hat?
The fall-over-and-get-chucked-out-of-a-taxi hat. The hat
rubbing his left ear and complaining he's misunderstood.
The hat saying *Go from here. Go home
to Little Miss Sugarplum who loves you very much
despite the constant smell of burning in the room.*
The hat orders a red wine and a red stripe.
Hat's name shouted from the top deck of a 57 bus.
The hat a voice in the night saying *I'm lonely*.
The hat considers suicide but it is not yet
his last resort. The hat transformed, redeemed
at last by the all healing properties of love.

My kingdom for a hat. Le hat c'est moi.
The ageing hat. The hat on a park bench
in the autumn of his days. The hat with a habit.
The hat studying his profile in the mirror.
The hat awake, aware, conscious, a sentient being
contemplating all the other mysteries of the universe,
wondering to himself *do you suppose there is*
a finite number of stars? The hat as holy writ.
The hat feels disinclined to go to evensong.
The hat rushed into hospital for emergency surgery.
The hat fallen on hard times, the hat with the blues.
The hat suffering from a hefty dose of paranoia.
The schizophrenic hat off his trolley,
out of his pram, two cups short of a tea-set.
The hat's seasonal transhumance through the Alps.
The hat helping the police with their enquiries.
The hat that died in the service of his country.
The hat brought down by insurrection and shot.
The hat sentenced to life for bloody murder.
The hat handing in his keys to the desk clerk
saying *c'est la vie mon cher ce n'est que rien.*
The homeland of the hat, green rolling hills
and the far river sparkling in the sunlight,
the hat remembers, the hat is in love, he says
I promise I will take you there, my beloved,
my woman of the hats, you who are my dream,
my gift my vision all my inspiration my love
amongst the white tongues of the arum lilies.
The hat's dream life. The hat's dark secrets.
The hat's prayer. The hat at his rutting.
The hat's occasional sexual peccadilloes.
The hat gets his rocks off. The hat purrs
with pleasure and pours himself a large Glenlivet.
The life and times and further adventures of a hat.
The hat dressed to the nines and going on the razzle.
The hat's programme for reform of the judiciary.
The hat's codicil to his last will and testament.
The hat's last territorial demand on Europe.
The hat as the currency of the Common Market.
The ghosts of dead hats. The hat in exile.
†I.M. Monsieur Hat, R.I.P. Requiescat in pace.

The hat gone to his just reward in hat heaven,
joined the great architect, kicked the bucket.
The wild hats hooting in the woods.
The hats that have no homes to go to.
hats who have changed their names for immigration.
The alienated hat. The blunt-spoken hat,
the ey-by-gum hat, the bugger-you-anyway hat,
the hat calling a hat a hat speaking his mind
and doing as he would like to be done by.
The hat sleeping it off in the ditch.
The last hat on the Yukon. The hat's death in Venice.
Superhat. Hat's last ride. Exit hat left.
The hat's memories of an idyllic childhood.
The hat will now reminisce for fifteen minutes.
The hat considers his options and draws up a plan.
The hat wins the Nobel Prize. The hat gets the OBE.
The hat packs his bags and moves to Amsterdam.
The hat going into a sulk. The hat in recession.
The hat swears innocence on his mother's grave.
The hat sitting down to a fine fish supper.
The hat saying *so who's been sleeping in my bed?*
The hat saying *I spy with my little eye.*
The hat switching channels. The hat movie.
The hat in a bag. The hat lost in the city.
The hat going down the pub to get drunk again.
Hat's story: I was married once, my sunflower
I called her, *come in* I said *under my broad brim.*
*under my high crown, come in love and I will warm
your cold innards.* She was pretty, we were madly in love.
So much for my perception of reality.
She ran off with the captain of the Woolwich Free Ferry
singing *sanfairyann my hairy little spider*
leaving me weeping bitter tears into my billycock.

The hat was no longer in my court.
The hat was now firmly on the other foot.
The hat was now put before the horse
that was now of a very different colour.
The hat hit the fan. The hat with egg all over its face.
The hat up hat creek as we say hereabouts
without a paddle, or *that hat won't hunt.*
Gnashings and wailings. Salt tears.

Lamentations throughout the Republic of Hats,
Beethoven on the radio, state mourning.
I learned the watched hat never boils,
to let sleeping hats lie, turn the other hat,
never count my hats before they hatch,
and that every hat has a silver lining.
Heyho I say who needs the aggravation?
Time to say *goodnight Comrade Vodka.*
I guess I made my hat and so must wear it.
So now I walk on the sunny side of the hat.
And I say plenty more where that came from,
there's still rivers and music and birds,
sunrise and sunset, sunlight and moonlight
and the sunstruck wind dabbed water on the mere.

Go tell the honey ant

The scavenger ants trek through the forest,
each day an exact slice of the compass.
They eat everything and they spare nothing
in that sector. They are out there,
I hear them with their black flags.

There are the slaves and there are the slavemakers,
toughs who spray propoganda substance
turning their victims onto each other,
and they make off with the eggs. These are the slaves.
They do all the work around here.

That's how it is in the ant universe.
Nothing can change it. But how would you like
to be pumped into a bag of glucose and water
hung from the ceiling against lean times?
Upside down. That's some career plan.

As for the bear grubbing in the bleak winter
of the bears, he's not interested in this
but in the rare sharp sweetness on his tongue.
He blinks. If I were you the bear in me says
I'd stick to sweet things, especially honey.

Columbus to Isabella

My ships are beached at Guincho,
furthest west into the ocean
and alas we are at war with the neighbours.

At the far limits of the sea
islands rose on the sky's edge,
where we landed, sea sore,

myself wearier than the rest
in all that muttering crew
eager to unship me and turn back.

200 nights I did not sleep
in my bunk nor change clobber,
bad meat and wormy bread

and all on my own dead reckoning
shortening the miles in the log,
reading birds and weeds in the sea

out where the pole star wandered
and the earth's shape was a pear
such as may lie before you, Lady.

The natives are mild and naked,
fit to be your servants
and receive Christ's Blood.

The gold is always further off,
west towards the falling sun,
silver as it pours into the sea.

Days on Dog Hill

A season of loose connections, bells
and weddings through the rainy summer.
I woke with my head in a crock,
I had dreamed of nothing.

I'm into town and out, down the hill
and up again, muttering *waggontruss,*
windbrace, through the tall woods
along the old pack road that no longer goes anywhere,

and like the windy leaves never still,
always on the way to some thought
lost in the traffic and the chatter,
the town below fading into voices off,

a hammer's knock travelling beyond itself,
a man shouting his name over and over,
lives made from the sounds they make.
These things do not connect:

a yellow flower from a far off country,
linked hearts cut in a tree's side,
sussura of pigeon wings, an animal threshing
the undergrowth, scribble of bird song

here, here, and your secret names for me –
Old Paint, Wild Root, Scissorbill. I dreamed
the ridge and these massed dark roots of the yews,
anger like a sudden wind. Wild root.

Here

I point to where the pain is, the ache
where the blockage is. Here.
The doctor shakes his head at me.
he says, I have that, we all have.

They put the wire in again, on the monitor
I watch the grey map of my heart, the bent
ladder of the spine that outlasts it.
How does it feel? they ask. Here?

I am moving away down the long corridors
of abandoned trolleys, the closed wings
of hospitals, rooms full of yellow bedpans
and screens and walker frames, fading out

into nothing and nothing at all, as we do,
as we all do, as it happens, and no one
can talk of it. Here, where the heart
dies, where all the systems are dying.

Night at the Blind Beggar

Easy-peasy they said, a simple job,
money for old rope. Here's a drink.
Go to the Blind Beggar in Whitechapel
between this hour and this hour.

Sink a slow thoughtful pint or two,
a tough young bucko in his suit and tie,
out for the evening on a mission,
the bystander with the job of seeing nothing.

A quiet night, the light fading, traffic
on the High Street, music on the jukebox.
Then at 8.30 Ronnie walks in with a Mauser
and blows a man's head all over the room.

Hadn't bargained for that.
Not that sort of drink.
Our man sees everything and nothing.
That's it he's out of there.

Jumped the District Line, at Paddington
the first train anywhere took him west
into an ordinary life: job, mortgage,
wife, kids, the years becoming more years.

Except the long days and longer nights
of all the rest of him are spattered
by the bits of brain on the wall
and blood over his white shirtfront.

This is his tale of how he got lost.
Dogget he says into the strange silence
he inhabits, the question mark as ever
slung around his shoulder. *Dog ate my dinner.*

The gracenote

Saturday night I'm on the Broadway,
round my own neck of the woods
listening for the numbers knowing
I'll have none of them that win.

Fourth pub left of the tube stop,
I'm in Murphy's where one of us
has a very bad cough, my mate says
she left me with just one chopstick,

I was one chopstick short of a pot noodle.
Most times it's like this, a strange
normality where I'm agawp, always,
a good listener is all of it, mimic

with an ear cocked for the gracenote –
always a nice touch though you don't want
too many gracenotes in any one place,
and I tell you all this for nothing.

I'm the starling on the wire, giving it
with all his harsh repertoire of cries,
some of them his own, some borrowed,
some blue, none of them ever repaid –

bits of magpie song and blackbird,
owl's voice, sometimes in a tone
recognisably human a single word:
habitually, habitually, habitually.

Narrow Road, Deep North

From the northbound train
white flecks on the brown ploughland
like flakes of fine snow –

they are birds, gulls,
suddenly flying. Across
winter fields somehow

I missed the white horse
on the hill that was boyhood,
all of it gone now.

Playing fields some place
that was some place once, goal posts
moved and again moved.

I'm on the run, hours,
days of the one bitter thought
on the narrow road

to my life's deep north,
in my pocket a ticket:
ADULT. ADMIT ONE.

Ah this long rocking
as the landscape turns to frost,
lulling me to sleep,

weeping and weeping
over the north, for my dead,
for all my lost ones,

they who will not come
my way again, them we won't
see again, ever.

The dry northern air,
the white wind will sort it out,
and the rain, the rain.

And everywhere birds
in a glitter of flying,
the landscape dancing.

At Culloden larks
that are dust in the tall air,
black flags of the crows.

Barefoot some, kilted,
charging through juniper, thorns,
thistles, their faces

set to the wind, sleet,
shrapnel, grapeshot, bayonets,
Cumberland's well trained

Hessian butchers –
hungry and down hearted, fell
all the wild flowers

of Scotland. Exeunt
clansmen, croftsmen, fishermen.
Bonnie Prince Dickhead,

says Billy, days away
on Skye, in the old mates' club,
and a dram to go.

Ah, water. The sunset
a riot. The far islands
where clouds are mountains

under deep white snow,
and the Hebridean *yes*
begins *no, no, no,*

and *no* again *no*
till the *yes* of it at the
sentence's finish:

aye a wee dram then.

This is for you Jim,
whose garden is the battlefield.
This is for you, Con,

that you stay upright
and vertical in Tarbert,
this god forsaken

hole. That the Wee Free
tether the goat, the rooster,
that the seventh day

is all cold meat, is
fact friend, *in the Good Black Book*
you will find mention

of boats but never
a bicycle. Things the heart
will no longer hold,

and bursts with, thoughts
on the waves and the west wind,
the long birds overhead,

heron, Brent Goose, swan,
their distant migrations,
continents their shores.

The light off the cliffs
climbing out of the dull sea
into rainclouds.

The best monuments
belong to the defeated,
and always anyway

and after a while
all the bartenders look alike
and your man goes off

the rails, *refreshments*
sounds in his ear like *fresh mints*
and on the rolling

bar on the rocking
boat asking for chewing gum
what he hears: *tuna*.

Let the light bleed out.
Let there be me and the landscape
and the moon, dreamer

when the dream goes out
into the next and the next,
following the tongue,

the eye, lone white house
on the hilltop, why don't I
live there?

I ran away to
Scotland, the people there to
see, and found a pound

was as round and soon
spent, home again home again,
jiggety-jig.

Ah but the cold clean
air of the mountains, water,
Callanish sunlight.

And again gulls' cries,
tern, bittern, the heart's last blips
on the monitor.

Time to go home.

The yellow dock gate
comes down and the town bell rings
two, two. From the dock

a woman calls her farewells
to her man and a voice shouts
Kenny, Kenny, but

it ain't me Sunshine,
we roll in the water's heave
on *The Isle of Mull,*

on passage, the land
fading to mist and distance,
on the dark water

black snouts of dolphins,
up from their own deep places,
breathing in ours.

Blue Prague: the worst you can say in Czech

It's true I desire to go far away
and mutter to myself in the wind,
taking the long train of myself off,
lost among strangers and distances.

If I called myself now on the phone
my voice would say I'm not at home just now
and what I then called now would now be then,
every moment its own in another time zone of the heart.

But no I was never in Prague, never got lost
in its blowsy statuary, never visited
the House of the Bell, nor drank the absence of absinthe,
never ate the Executioner's Special.

I was never the King's Jew.
I was a limping man on a stick
with a broken eyeglass, just
an old *dedek* with his tobacco.

Nic moc, no big deal. The city
a blue rainy haze of lights, *Strasne dobry,*
awesome, a wolf wind howling over the tiles,
crack of flags like gunfire, bells.

Nekecam. I met a tall man walking
with a tiny cactus in his fist.
The chambermind will bring the cattle.
Would you like grilled meat on the needle?

Messages: among the scrambled stones
and bladed upright Hebrew a folded note:
let the hatred cease. Crows overhead
sawing the air, the souls of ancient rabbis.

Doprdele, the worst you can say,
lost in blue toothy Prague.
*Sere medved lese? May all your sons
be bartenders. Nosi papez legracni klebouk?*

JOURNEY WITHOUT MAPS

1 *Night train*

The moon's wide open mouth, its
thin light over fields and woods
that could be anywhere, distant names
of cities chanted on the speakers –
their two notes *born free, born free.*

Outside the same night: lit windows
flying backwards through the dark,
the streetlamps of little towns
lighting empty roads no one
is walking home, late, tipsy.

And in a flash of sudden neon
a tall crane in a field of wrecked cars.
It is the night of old shoes, their mouths
slackly open: *where now brother,*
how long ago was yesterday,
how many days until tomorrow?

2 *September distance*

A blur of birches. Borders
that are more than what you feel there,
wind rushing the reeds, long wing
of wild geese flying south, sunflowers,
poppyheads and milkweed, forest,
mile after mile the tall fields of maize,
the long plains measuring the distance,
west to east autumn yellowing the leaves.

It is a place called Russian Horse,
a place called Shoemaker in Iron County,
a city of bells and crippled gypsies,
the Gold Boys in and out the bars.

The streetsweeper sifts his broom
for flakes of fallen gold.
The dancing whore in Goat Town calls
oh tonight I want a man between my legs.

3 **What Feri said**

In the far distant relation
between Finnish and Hungarian

one sentence is the same
and only one and though

we don't know what it is
we know it is about fish,

a live fish swims underwater.
And in Vogul a sentence

the same as ours it says
twenty women's horses go on ahead.

4 *Glimpse*

of a man tapping his finger
on a map: *here, I live here,*
not much of a place, a crossroads
with a light that doesn't work,
a store that doesn't sell much
and a closed petrol station,
nowhere in particular but we think
it's the centre of the universe:
Podunkstadt that was before the wars,
thereafter called Amnesza.

After the changes the beer is better
but still undrinkable. Things are not good
but they are not unhopeful. Here
we have the best of everything
but you can't have any of it.

5 *Flatlands*

This is another place I won't remember
somewhere on the great plain
of long byres and tall wells and sky
where I have been travelling fast
with that far shine on the road ahead
and the wind over me, at night the cars
with their lights trembling on the highway,
as if the stars were passing through us.

Moments that are snapshots, coins slipped
in a beggar's cup, a one-legged man
on a bicycle with a broken umbrella
waiting at the crossroads that are
always unlucky places, the burials
of lost travellers and victims,
beside the memorial's unreadable epitaph
eaten over by lichen and rain.

6 *Closed border, Slavonia*

Over there the flag of one country
blowing in the wind of another
beyond the closed checkpoint:
fields, river, birchscrub, the same.

This is the border where the road runs out
into a tractor trail of snowy mud
to the last house by the wire,
and all the dogs are barking.

Nothing between me and the wind,
tall reeds and border fences,
here to say I've been here,
take a snapshot and turn home,

a traveller with his keepsakes –
a man's bone from an old battlefield,
a bent bullet from Mostar,
weary with the weight of my self.

7 *TV in the East*

On SKY and SAT late night images
passing for desire and its flesh,
the play of light wherein they kiss
and soft things flutter to the floor,
a mouth begins its snail of a descent
to the promise of a breast and cut
to the commercial: all the lives
we may not want and cannot have.

And on the Russian channel mirror script:
mountains, a place far to the east
of open sky and early snow, a swift
upland river and slow drummers,
chants, horses and horsemen, women
in a long line through windy smoke,
led by an old man wearing skins,
on his head the antlers of a deer.

8 *Waking in Heroes' Park*

Too many days counting coup on the borders:
countries sucking on their stones,
some gone rusty in the rain,
another sulking on its wounds.

Markets and stations, crossings
where the police jump on the vagrants
and the fugitives, everyone's a suspect,
everyone an item in their career moves.

In Heroes' Park I wake to white noise
and the world sailing its ocean of dirty air,
across a bridge men carrying planks,
copper pipe and scaffolding, tea kettles,

sheets of clear glass. And through
the autumn trees a line of bright
schoolchildren, babbling like a river,
where I wake, dreaming of chickens.

Moscow dogs

Sasha says:
all the chairs in here are broken
though some are more broken than others.

Outside over the garbage cans visited
every few minutes by the old and the poor
a white plastic bag drifts on the updraughts

so delicately, riding the air,
settles on the new leaves of the cotton tree
just above the steps to the door that never opens.

The only reply:
three legs good, four legs better.
I want the words for dogs, huge, loose on the streets

but the only Russian I know is *da, niet, voda, pivo,*
vodka, spasibo, dosvidanya: yes, no, water,
beer, vodka, thankyou and goodnight.

Horrowshow: very good. *Spiceybar*: thankyou.
Watch our for the dogs.
To say *I love you* say *yellow blue vase.*

All the old fear lurks on the stairs
all the way down the elevator shaft
in this Stalinist wedding-cake block of flats,

it blows on the dust of the streets,
on everyone's shoes, in everyone's bones.
Watch our for the dogs.

HUNGARIAN QUARTET

The night anywhere

is just a car choking into life and idling
as he nurses it to warmth, the window ice
melting as he buckles in, the flare
his lighter makes in the inner dark
and she chiding his late drinking,
hoping he will drive slowly on the black roads,
and he will let her sleep tonight.

There is a man's far away shout, a woman's cry.
It could be anywhere: the cold night stars
burning overhead, the silence of the snow,
a horizon of dogs recalling how they ran in packs
long ago though this flat border country.
It could be here in the Bacska running south
with the great river down to lost Vojdovina.

It's late, after palinka and fisherman's soup.
Then for hours the thump of the bowling balls
the local skinheads and the Serbs downstairs
roll half the night between long telephone calls
to somewhere far away. It could be now.
It could be anywhere in this northern winter
before sleep. It could be anyone's song.

Sándor the poet

Meet Sándor the gypsy. He is a poet
in his own kingdom, under the reeds.
Today he is building his winter house.
This is his pig. Thankyou he says.

Thankyou for coming to see me.
Would you like to marry my daughter?
You are a rich man from the West. Be kind to her.
Buy her chocolate and pink champagne.

Someone is shoving a wire through a pig's nose.
Someone is revving a motorbike
up and down the dusty alley. When the screaming stops
you hear water pouring from the pump,

you hear the wind over the waste and the reeds
where his people live by the old Russian barracks
at Kiskunmajsa. They could move in there
but the government, the government.

The bitter eyes of the gypsies,
empty pockets, empty glasses. Soon
it may be time to go to jail again.
Soon again winter, when some will die

in this village without a name.
A special tribe he says, their leathery
wee women are blue eyed yellow haired
daughters of the Red Army, 1944.

Namyo he shrugs: doesn't work.
He waves at the flies, complaining
you see how it is here with us
the Cigany? Look at the flies on the bread.

And picks up his instrument and plays
a lament for the ancient distance,
at night a sky burning with stars,
every one of them Hungarian.

Alma the apple. *Roka* the fox.
The leaves are drifting from the trees.
Soon will come the bleak zima of the pusta.
Thankyou for coming to see me.

Michi's song

I will sing one song
from Novi Sad. But this
this is not a song.

The words: difficult, different.
I can't remember: la la la.
Oh my love.

My beloved landscape and the landscape of my beloved.
I was born to it.
I should die there.

Each night the phone rang.
Sometimes silence, breathing. Or a man
cursing in Serbian:

why don't you go?
You have a wife, children,
we can kill them.

You we will impale.
Land I was born to.
This is not a song.

Dmitri's song

I will sing now the lost song
in the lost voice from the lost time

if I can find it
if I can find where I left it

the old song from the old time
of an old man who is young again

ah but always

something is wrong in exile
and the heart is bloody always

THE SHADOW OF GOD

I am Suleyman, sultan of sultans, sovereign of sovereigns, distributor of crowns to the lords of the surface of the globe.

I am Suleyman, the Shadow of God on earth, Commander of the Faithful, Servant and Protector of the Holy Places.

I am Suleyman, ruler of the two lands and the two seas, sultan and padishah of the White Sea and of the Black, of Rumelia, of Anatolia, of Karamania, and of the land of Rum I am Rum Kayseri.

I am lord of Damascus, of Aleppo, lord of Cairo, lord of Mecca, of Medina, of Jerusalem, of all Arabia, of Yemen and of many other lands which my noble forefathers and illustrious ancestors (may God brighten their tombs) conquered by the force of their arms and which my august majesty has subdued with my flaming sword and my victorious blade.

I am Sultan Suleyman Han, son of Sultan Selim Han, son of Sultan Bayezid Han.

I am Suleyman. To the east I am the Lawgiver. To the west I am the Magnificent.

*

84

Suleyman. In his dream the far world
is a basket of heads at his saddlebow,
sunlight's flash on the edges of blades
raised in his name to the dim horizon:
I am Suleyman. At the end of Ramadan,
in the spring of the year that will send
his quarrelsome soldiery north again
Suleyman rises from sleep, consults maps,
glancing up glimpsing the evening star
low in the cobalt canopy of the day's end
caught in the thicket of the new moon's
upturned horns, and takes that for his omen.
That year as every year war is a season,
war is a fetva, a jihad waged on all
the unreconciled world of unbelievers
beyond the gaze of the Magnificent.

That year his beard points west again
to the domain of war: glimpse of far hills,
country scoured flat by the rivers, the beasts
are deer and wild pig leaving their tracks
on the soggy waterlands, on the scrubland
thistles, milkweed, juniper, vines,
the eyes of the tall white birches
glimpsed through the pines. The birds
are swift, hawk, crow and kingfisher,
the little seedeaters, the buzzards
sentinels on his way, the storks
from their round high nests in the wind
glance after him, the pheasant's stutter,
the owl's stare in his tracks, the woodpecker
tapping in the dark light of the woods,
the shrike pinning his dinner to a thorn.

The Lawgiver, Suleyman, whom the Prophet
favour and posterity long remembers,
goes out of the city to his war camp.
He hoists the six black horsetails of his flag,
unwraps the forty silk shawls from the black
sacred banner of Mohammed and raises it,
and from all the heaven protected empire
of dur ul Islam come the levies, sipahiler,
akincilar, seğmenler, tüfekçiler, azaplar,
topçular, yeni çeriler, tribesmen and the wild
bowmen of the steppes, the half naked dervish
not counted into the muster, one hundred thousand
dreaming of loot, calling his name, *Suleyman,*
taking the roads north, Constantinople to Belgrade
and the rough tracks beyond into the wastes
of the unbelievers, the mire of the infidel.

In his journal there is rain, endless rain,
day after day the grey slanting downpour,
vague cloudy horizons and the sky's flood.
And bitter winds. 80 days on the march
in the downpour on no road that is a road
driving the great train north, 80 nights
pitched in the sheeted rain, slithering
with horses and camels and weaponry
in the black Balkan mud of the flood plains,
left of the river between the rivers
in that year of the rain. The beasts
are deer and boar and wolf, the birds
hawk and butcher bird, black cormorant
low over his black shadow on the river,
crows in a black storm overhead, or perched
on a stump, watching the way God watches.

Ropes split, the big guns sink in the bogs,
the cries of horses and men no one hears,
merely the dead born to die in the muck
for the enlargement of empire and the word
of the Prophet, may God's smile ever rest on him,
for the enrichment of some, enslavement of some,
somewhere in the mapless country of the rain,
crushed by the wheels, some lost in sinkholes,
the ropes falling away from their hands
and last of them the O of their upturned
mouths calling his name: *Suleyman, Suleyman.*
The names of the days are rain and wind,
the names of the rivers run into each other.
Up the Danube day after day 800 boats
weigh upwind upstream on the downcoming
agua contradictionis beyond which the barbarians.

Under the six black horsetail standard,
under the sacred banner the horse army
lugs its stores and its guns northward
into the oncoming rain and the clutter of mud
and the wind in their faces: cavalry, artillery,
sharpshooters, musketmen, soldiers, raiders,
shaggy Tatar horsemen, all dreaming of rape.
300 cannon through the marshes, some lost,
the horses straining, the whips, no roads,
no bridges in all this nowhere of mud,
tracks that run to dead ends, watery graves,
roads running off into water, marsh paths
learned at a blade's edge and goodbye
the quick blood, always eager to be off,
goodbye the names hawk and buzzard and heron,
the names Sava and Drava mean nothing now.

Suleyman. The bared teeth of the horses,
their necks rear from the reeds, screaming
as horses scream, men scream, the rain falls.
Imprint of reeds on the sky lances on the wind,
lancemen and horsemen. The birds are shrike,
buzzard, crow, the owl falling on its shadow,
the harrier's underspread wingspan two skulls
on the grey light rising on the sky, the rivers
Sava and Drava and Danube though the names
mean nothing to him. Problems with stores,
problems with water, questions of powder,
fuel for the cooking pots, meat, some warmth
in the long shivering rain, shaving the rust
from their blades, sword, knife, sabre, spear,
matchlock and carbine, guns lugged down roads
built of reeds, the stores rotting away.

The sodden saddlesore army of divine light,
fractious and lice-ridden and chilled to the bone,
crying *Suleyman Suleyman,* those running before
crying *Suleyman Suleyman,* the Magnificent.
He is crossing the Drava on a golden throne
from the domain of peace to the domain of war.

                  To Mohacs
in the marshlands, still in the pouring rain,
August 29th, 1526, where those summoned
and hastily gathered died in thousands
in the space of a moment the chronicler
scribbles, in the safety of distance,
cruel panthers in a moment to hell's pit.

That day the guns chained wheel to wheel,
smoke and the cries of men and horses,
the knights shot from their saddles, armour
dragging them into the mire, the hooves
stamping them in, the infantry butchered,
in the space of a moment the swift
routine of retreat, slaughter and rout,
the space of a moment. No prisoners,
the wails of the wounded, the dying, becks

brimmed with blood, and the young king
thrown from his horse, drowned in his breastplate.
Thereafter Suleyman recalls he sat on the field
in the pouring rain on his glittering throne
to the long applause of his army: *I am*
Sultan Suleyman Han, son of Sultan Selim Han,
son of Sultan Bayezid Han. The shadow of God.

And they butcher the captives, dig the pits
to bury their own brave dead, horses and men,
30 thousand whose last rainy day was this,
and the other dead lie in the rain, or scatter
their bones in the wetlands and the reedgrass.
Whatever birds pecked out their eyes
their names are no matter nor the stream
they drowned in nor the name of the planet
whose soft brown body they shovelled in after.
Thereafter the land burns and the churches,
thereafter women and slaves and silver.
And thereafter, pronounces the historian,
his quill's tip brushing his cheek, his point
squeaking over the page, the lamp's glint
on his inkhorn: *the long Turkish night,*
the tomb of the nation, dug in the rain.

In the space of a moment, in the centuries
moments pile into, leaf over leaf,
season by season as the winters pass
and the wars roll over and the borders shift
it is ploughland, old bones surfacing
at the hoe's edge and the plough's iron,
scapulae and vertebrae rising in a flat
wide fenced country laid open to the wind,
prowled by the tractors of the collectives
and the same wandering birds, black earth
through white snow, wind beaten scarecrow
and the white silence of another winter.
It is a museum of bones in the thick boney
stew of each other, where some bird sings
in the evergreens and a boy rings a bell
in the long white silence that follows.

It is a field of poles upright at a pit's rim,
carved into cruel faces, chiselled in grimaces,
spiked, helmeted, horned, a ragged line of posts
that are totems of men straggling off into trees,
some aslant, the long necks of horses
rearing from snow. They are flail and bludgeon
and battleaxe, calvaries of yokes and the bows
of the swift horsemen, the trailed arms
of the willow tree. They are the crescent moon
and the star, the cross, the crown, the turban
and the tarboosh, gnarled glances of soldiers,
the figures of dead men rising from the earth,
Suleyman with a basket of heads at his pommel
and the dead king Lajos in his blue bonnet.

Overhead the high jets in the clear blue
corridor of cloudless sky above Serbia,
flying the line of the great rivers
whose names are the same though the names
of the empires and the nations shift
on the maps. South of here, not far,
in the debateable lands of the warring states
the bones are again rising in the mud.

The wooden cock crows from his wooden post.
In the clear dry air a bell rings.

*

A bell rings. In the town the dogs bark
and all night again the banging of boats
on the river and the thud of drifting ice
on their hulls and the slapping of waves.

Always dogs, beyond gates, over walls,
loose on the streets, howling to the far
flat ring of the world's edge of woods,
rivers, barns, border posts.

Wolfhounds, manhounds, pit bulls,
mutts, mastiffs and mongrels bawling
at cats, cars, bells, footsteps, wind
in the winter trees, the yellow moon.

Each with his patch to scratch, each
his yard to guard, each with his own
view of the world, his own particular opinion
he will not give up easily.

Wars begin with this and end whimpering.
They begin with the squabbles of neighbours
and end in the baying of men: what's mine
is mine. And yours is mine also.

And someone has backed into the lamppost again,
someone has knocked over the empty bottles,
someone has burst into drunken tuneless song
on the late street and set all the dogs off.

Someone has been beating his wife again,
broken all the crockery in the kitchen,
woken the kids and the curs and the old wounds,
slammed the door shut, kicked the gatepost.

And gone off to the river to think it all out,
contemplate drowning himself at last
as all round in his reeling skull
in the great dark the dogs bark.

*

Very fast very slow this music
a lament from the villages
a music come down from the mountains
called across rivers across plains:
ah no joking and no joking
a gift for the kolo, bridegroom
the thieves they are singing
dance my love dance faster
faster till we fall down.

The reedgrass that will be thatch
first snowy fields turned in the plough.
a line of trucks in a white field
waiting for grain not yet sown:
end of the winter quarter
end of the season of craving
the river's ice drifting south
snow collapsing from the buildings:
the days of the death of King Winter.

The *Busojárás.*

Time to take to the streets
wearing the skins of beasts
masks years in the making offspring
of the old whisperers in the hearth
kin to the devotees of trees
and certain stones and all rivers
lord of the vines and beasts
our lady of the wild things the old gods
who never made it into heaven.

Busos.

They step out of the unwritten
the unremembered out of Illyria
out of the south the dark the flight
and the distant remembrance of panic
the horned hoof footed hard drinking
god of the shepherds. They step out
through the winter streets in masks
horns in sheepskins and old bandoliers
with their bells and their rattles.

Busos.

With their antlers tall in the skins
of beasts belled shaggy moustache men
huge with their clubs and horns
wild in their tall wooden masks
coming on from the distance
all the years they have travelled
out of the unlettered the *agrapha*
the history of the forgotten
the long shadows of the lost gods.

At noon they have crossed the river
they have taken the streets
filled with organised riot
the ruckus of men in the male dance
the clatter and rattle of flails
the interminable clanging of bells
rain clanking into buckets
in mockery taking their ways
through the orders of anarchy.

Busos.

Fierce and yet not fierce
joking and yet not joking
this is the management of chaos:
the war of the great ratchets
the battle of the bells upright animals
striding through the streets
through the cold falling sunlight
in a wild skirling music
bearing the skulls of animals.

Busos.

Others come as veiled hooded women
a brown friar another the devil
a joker in a Russian tank mask
a Groucho Marx an Austrian helmet.
And these others ghosts in dirty sheets
rags sackcloth and ashes and stocking masks
bunched in knots of impudent silence
young men scattering the girls
the dead risen from the dead.

Centuries ago the traveller
Evliya Çelebi warned his far flung
wandering countrymen of the masked
madmen of Mohacs in the marshland
in their shaggy jackets and bells
and their faceless faces:
they are devils devils
in the place of devils
no one should go there.

In their own legend of themselves
they chased the Turks out of town
in terror. In the ill-disciplined
shaggy masked half drunk ranks
among pitchforks and whirling clubs
the carved severed head on a stick
of a janissary, moustache top knot skull
goes round and round in the racket
and the gathering fire and the dusk.

How years ago they were fearless
in the place of defeat and rose again
how years ago a pig's blood painted
a cross in the town square and how
the masks stained in animal blood
and the wild cries and the kolo
was their resistance. How once
they were one with the beasts
one with men one with the gods.

Rutting and butting as beasts
sticks for pricks bells balls
and under the mask is another
and another they are Busos
three days of the year Busos
parading their ragged squads
to the square where the cannon
from that year of the rain
thunders mud and rags and smoke.

Busos.

Come nightfall on the third day
of marching and mayhem and music
that is Shrovetide the fire's lit
in the square. King Winter is dead
carted off in a coffin and burned.
On the coffin in flowery
Hungarian script: *it's sold,*
our country, it's sold, we have
nothing left but our father's pricks.

Where does this music come from?
an old woman asks. From all round her
from everywhere from earth
from the wind from the long turned
furrows of defeat the old sorrow
the old joy the songs
of the long gone into the dark.
It's sold, our country,
and all the thieves are laughing.

Time to march one last time
on the town and burn winter
with bells and cannon and fire
round and around the tottering square
masked men and horses the music
round and round the kolo
the dancing of the hairy men
and winter goes up in the flames
the tall smoke climbing the sky.

Busos.

The sliver of moon the first star
on the pale blue flag of the sky
as the sparks flare and die. At the edge
of the embers of memory the borders
of hearing: bells laughter a child
a cough girls singing the swift music
in the ashes of the evening
wisps of voices at a distance
in that far off language.

WIRE THROUGH THE HEART

Where the scythe has been

This is the music of no music.
You have to listen hard if you're listening at all
to hear it out on the wind through the aspens,
faint as far off bells, as birds
on the edges of hearing, dogs in another country,
wolves working their way across the horizon.

It begins among the smashed stones
of some old Jewish graveyard glimpsed
in passing on the long roads somewhere,
some star in the window of a place
selling auto parts, a faint air
round the bare brickwork of a dead synagogue
in some town whose name you no longer remember,
where is no shul any more, no Sabbath,
no dark sidelocked men arriving on carts
with their shawled women, their solemn
children in long coats perched
like chickens, where is no kaddish said
for the millions who never came back,
where isn't ten together who can say it.

The music of where music has been:
only the tall windblown grasses
in the abandoned yard that will fall
to someone's else's scythe
to the descant of bird song
before the summer's over –
the soft sigh of the blade.

Signed sealed & delivered
(for Erzsébet, Kisszelmenc, Ukraine)

This is your permission.
Your licence. Keep it safe somewhere,
these words will get you through.
You will need them to pick herbs
by the border wire, and a handful of flowers
to put on your mother's grave
in the village where you were born
in the other country whose steeple
you can see from your yard's end.

To get there you will need this paper,
and again when you come back to say
you have been there. You will need
these words to say you have read them.

This is your permission to be someone,
anyone, a person called Kovacks
who says it's all right to love someone,
to excess even, to go crazy,
to piss in the street, go to jail,
to one day die and briefly be remembered
best for the side of you that stood in light
at the gate of your house in spring
just before the sun went down, considering
the acacia blossoms and the onions
and your own diminishing options.

This is your permit, your passport
to the other side of anywhere.
Signed, sealed, delivered,
dated this day vaguely in May.

Of course, the signature's illegible
and on the wrong side of the paper.
And the rubber stamp cut from a bar of soap
was stolen long ago. And in any case
as to delivery there are no stamps,

100

the post office became a nightclub,
and the postman if he's been paid
since January, and if you still
have a letter box, he might just deliver it.

Maybe.

The Secret Police

(for Zelei Bori)

They are listening in the wires,
in the walls, under the eaves
in the wings of the house martins,
in the ears of old women,
in the mouths of children.

They are listening to this now.

So let's hear it for the secret police,
a much misunderstood minority.
After all, they have their rights,
their own particular ways of seeing things,
saying things, cooking things,
they too have a culture uniquely their own.

And we think
they should have their own state
where they could speak their own
incomprehensible tongues, write
their confessions, their unknown histories,
cultivate their habits of watching
by watching each other, and fly
their own flags there, at attention
on parade in their medals at their monuments
on their secret anniversaries, making speeches,
singing praises to the God of Paranoia.

And at the end of the day
bury their dead, publish their coded obituaries
of each other, and rest at last
in their own kind of peace, forever.

Intermezzo, Sub-Carpathia, May 97

There is a bird in here, an oriole perhaps,
a nightingale trying to get out still singing
across the border between sleep and waking,
bringing the dream along. Sometimes
a solemn joyful music from the church
in some village of black widows clutching
prayer books, the black crows of sorrow.
Then a high chant from the music school
in was it Munkacs?, and round the back
the strings tuning up, and once
in the muddy street of the gipsies
the boy's high soprano above accordion
and badly tuned fiddle.
                              Wind
around the small sandblown hills, the reeds.

In the vaults hacked deep in the rock
the cold wine sleeps, that will become
a sharp memory on the tongue, the cold
tug of the air on the body. Elsewhere,
Istvan the First sweeps bees from a honeycomb
with a long grey bird's wing, the bees drink
at the watertub and fill the air with sound,
honey spills into jars, one the beekeeper
gave me to sweeten my mornings, its gold light
shining here now on my windowsill.

In any case

The lives we live, always taking us
over some border, we spend our years
trying to get there, in the tracks
of the old migrations through the passes,
west and out from the land between the rivers
down the broken roads of the armies.

Everywhere old borders, countries slithering
on the maps, on their rafts of magma
never still for long. Everywhere memorials,
the dead of wars and Stalin's Terror
in these parts, the starry graves
of the drunk heroes of the Soviet Union,

and others unknown. Along
the roadsides crosses for those
who hit the brakes too soon, swerved,
hit a bus, burst into fire, went over
into the brown flood of the Tisza,
a bunch of fading plastic flowers.

We took the river road into the mountains
through the towns of closed factories,
where even the salt mines were shut,
a stork preening her ragged nest
on the tall brick factory chimney,
up through the high villages of the shepherds.

Fleeting: the fast river full of rain,
plank bridges hung over the flood,
wires and watchtowers over in Romania,
halfway up a steep impossible hill
a man in a blue shirt climbing to the sky,
the villages shifting into other tongues.

To the Tatar Pass of savage raiders
with no place to go back to. To the
Verecke Pass, where the seven tribes
of the people of the ten arrows came,

long ago though in any case the date
is debatable, the stone monument
lost in all the paperwork in far Kiev,

in any case unfinished. Up here the air's
foreign and thin, the first flash of lightning
among the peaks, the misty distance.
What of the 18,000 driven through here
in August 1941 to be shot on the other side
just for being Jews? What of the thousands

dead at Szolyva of cold and hunger,
typhus and TB and dysentry for being Hungarian?
For half a century no one could speak of them,
put chisel to stone. *Here* it says
on the boulder over the mass graves
Here one day will be a monument.

The materials in any case have been stolen.
I hear one man reading from the stone,
another say *here should be a monument*
to the unknown thief. Then wind again,
the mountain river rushing to its meeting
with the ocean, half a continent away.

Hutzul

Villages in the high valleys, a tall
long legged people, come early summer
they walk off into the distance,
grazing their sheep among the clouds,
making cheese in their high solitary huts
over the old tracks of the transhumance.

This must be one of their jokes,
this busted flush of a country
with its government of shadows
in leather jackets and shades.

This is another:
                    from peak to peak
across rocks and fast water, birdsong
and bleating and the far glitter of bells,
one Hutzul is asking another for news.

Haven't you heard? comes the voice
carried on the distance the sound travels:
The Russians have gone to the moon.

What, all of them?

No, just one of them.

So what's to shout about?

Heaven's dust

I would have sent you a postcard, love:
view of the castle on the river
that is all the names of this place:
Ungvar/Uzgorod. Dusty streets
hosed by rain, scrawny horses,
the market, old town, old doorways.
Faces of shepherds or a long shot
of the mountains, gipsy women
in red flowered dresses, the footbridge
over the river. A few snapshots
of desolation: an old woman selling
two toothbrushes, a lightswitch
and a heap of shrivelled radishes,
empty plinths where Lenin stood,
the biggest wolves in the world,
the old synagogue across the river.

But there are no postcards.
No stamps, no post office,
and in any case it would never reach you
bearing its message Oh I love you
from the collapsing country
across the shifting borders.

It would have said *Furthest point*
Europe from three seas/ the pole
of continentality/ 670 Km. equidistant
Adriatic Baltic Black Sea./ Oh
lovely River Uz/ thou givest me such a buzz/
Oh gorgeous River Ung/ thy praises we have sung
in good Slovak beer.
                    And who
would have thought in all the
siftings of the stars I'd be here,
an old man with his tobacco?
Surely we are all heaven's dust. All's well.

Border theatre

No, I am carrying no contraband,
no firearms, Kalashnikovs, missile launchers,
no drugs, no coils of copper wire from Minsk,
no nuclear materials, no body parts,
no bodies, no bullion, no known diseases.
Yes, I would like to leave your country now
and put its broken roads and rusty monuments
behind me, and Yes I'd like to leave
in less than the 36 hours it may take
for this performance on the border at Uzgorod.

Act One: *The first gate.* The actors
are police and tough leather men
who shake each others' hands, swap
cigarettes, their parts and uniforms
interchangeable, short of speech
and not much eye contact, men of few words
and blank faces and all they say is No. Wait.
What's happening is difficult to tell,
some drive up and drive away,
some wait hours, some straight through.

This for the first hour when suddenly
it's action time, we're in the cage
and in the second act called *Wait & See*
at the soldiers' gate where we wait,
wait, where nothing happens much, money
changes into money, a blue beer truck
passes for the second time and back,
guards mooching down the border strip
through vines, the watchtower watching,
flags snapping in the wind.

Hours more until it's hurry up and wait again
down the long hill of traffic, uniforms,
exhaust gas, another hour to the last act
and the exit and the exit stamp.

Yes, this is my own face, the one I usually wear
to these occasions, Yes this my bag,
Yes this my emergency tin of sardines.
And then we go. Not recommended.
A seven-hour performance all about itself,
and we say we're lucky. There's no applause.

Malenki robot

(for János, Nagyszelmenc, Slovakia)

'Over there in the other country
my sister had daughters I've seen once
in forty years, nor visited my dead.
It's too late now, they're poor there,

and here I'm just an old working man,
and the only thing left for me to do is die.

'These are my blunt carpenter's hands,
and this on their backs the frost
that gnawed them at Szolyva, three winters,
two years I was a prisoner there.
Monday I build doors, Tuesday put on roofs.
Roofs. Doors. My life. Vodka.
It was the priest told me to go,
three days he said, a little light work,
malenki robot, two years building roofs,
and that because I had a trade.
I survived wearing the clothes of those who died,
after a while I survived because I had survived,
and then came home and here the border.'

The wire runs through the heart, dammit,
therefore we will drink cheap Russian vodka
in János' kitchen, and later take a walk
down to the border and look back
into the other world, the village in the mirror
that is the other half of us, here,
where the street stops at the wire
and goes on again on the other side,
and maybe the gipsies will come to serenade us.

Ken Smith was born in 1938 in Rudston, East Yorkshire, the son of an itinerant farm labourer. He has worked in Britain and in America as a teacher, freelance writer, barman, magazine editor, potato picker and BBC reader, and has held writing fellowships at Leeds University, Kingston Polytechnic, and Clark University and Holy Cross, Worcester, Massachusetts. From 1985 to 1987 he was GLA writer-in-residence at Wormwood Scrubs prison. He received the Lannan Literary Award for Poetry in 1997, and a Cholmondeley Award in 1998. He lives in East London.

Smith's first book, *The Pity*, was published by Jonathan Cape in 1967, and his second, *Work, distances/poems*, by Swallow Press, Chicago, in 1972. Poems from these two collections and from a dozen other books and pamphlets published between 1964 and 1980 (including *Fox Running*) were brought together in his Bloodaxe Selected Poems, *The Poet Reclining* (1982; reissued 1989), which does not include work from *Burned Books* (1981) or his later Blood-axe titles. Ken Smith was the first poet to be published by Blood-axe, with his pamphlet *Tristan Crazy* in 1978.

In 1986 Ken Smith's collection *Terra* was shortlisted for the Whitbread Prize. In 1987 Bloodaxe published his collected prose, *A Book of Chinese Whispers*. His last four collections, *Terra* (1986), *Wormwood* (1987), *The heart, the border* (1990) and *Tender to the Queen of Spain* (1993) have all been Poetry Book Society Recommendations. His latest collection, *Wild Root*, is the Poetry Book Society Choice for autumn 1998, and has been shortlisted for the T.S. Eliot Prize.

In 1989 Harrap published *Inside Time*, Ken Smith's book about imprisonment, about Wormwood Scrubs and the men he met there. This was published in paperback by Mandarin in 1990.

Ken Smith was working in Berlin when the Wall came down, writing a book about East and West Berlin: this turned into *Berlin: Coming in from the Cold*, published by Hamish Hamilton in 1990 and in paperback by Penguin in 1991. He edited the anthology *Klaonica: poems for Bosnia* (Bloodaxe Books, 1993) with Judi Benson, and co-edited with Matthew Sweeney *Beyond Bedlam* (Anvil Press Poetry, 1997), a book of poems by mentally ill people.